HOW TO DEAL WITH DEM]

A POSITIVE APPROACH FOR COPING WITH THE EARLY STAGES OF DEMENTIA, ALZHEIMER'S AND VASCULAR DEMENTIA

By Jane Hanson

Published by: Mélanie Taylor Ebook Press
https://www.facebook.com/MelanieTaylorebooks

© Copyright 2014 Mélanie Taylor Ebook Press. All Rights Reserved. No part of this book may be reproduced in any form or by any means without the prior written permission of the publisher.

*****

For a FREE Colourful Daily Activity Guide especially designed by the author
Go to the enquiries page at
http://jaliart.com/contact.php

Thank you for down loading my book.
Please be kind and review this book on Amazon. I need your feedback to make the next one better.

*****

TABLE OF CONTENTS

Preface

About Author

Introduction

Chapter 1: What Are The Best Tactics For Dealing With Dementia?

Chapter 2: Do You Understand The Sufferer's Perspective?

Chapter 3: Can You Make Sense Of Your Time Together?

Chapter 4: What About You?

Chapter 5: I've Not Lost My Mind, It's Backed Up On Disk Somewhere

Chapter 6: What's The Science Behind These Activities?

Chapter 7: What Other Fun Activities Are There To Do In The Early Stages of Dementia?

Final Reflections

PREFACE

My intention in writing this book is to show that the world does not come to an abrupt halt when dementia is diagnosed – but rather that each day following diagnosis should be embraced and lived to the full. We are dealing here with the early stages of the disease, a time to continue with a happy and fulfilling life for as long as possible. As when any diagnosis is delivered to us, the temptation is to stop in our tracks and expect that our quality of life will become instantly poorer; it is easy to allow our spirits to drop and a 'worst case scenario' mindset to take over. So do try to keep positive, live for the day.

I tried as a carer to make each day richer for my aunt, who developed dementia in her 70's, as well as for my family: to keep the shutters of the mind open with sensory therapies, as well as a lot of laughter. I won't pretend that life was a bed of roses – but by recounting my story, I want to try to show that a different approach to life is possible for dementia sufferers and their carers, one that can be beneficial to all. Life changes, but can remain rich, even with new learning curves to negotiate.

I use the phrase "it worked for us" quite a lot, as we adapted our lifestyle to allow my aunt to be fully included and engaged in our family life. It was a journey that my family and I made together, one that made us stronger and more understanding of each other. We laughed and, at times, cried together, but we were "together" – a firm, supportive family unit.

So, live each day happily and see your cup as half-full, not half-empty – even as the dementia game sends you up the snakes and down the ladders.

ABOUT AUTHOR

Jane Hanson, a professional artist, started her working life in the teaching profession, before becoming quite an entrepreneur – running several city shops and then setting up and running a successful service company.

She now has an active life as singer, artist, writer and leader of a community group for those affected by dementia.

Very family orientated, Jane has cared for several family members, including her aunt Noreen, who lived with her and her family for many years and who developed dementia in her early 70s.

Together they travelled the dementia road and during these years developed a series of complementary therapies to heighten Noreen's senses.

It was while trialling art therapy with Noreen that Jane began to develop her own style of colour crystal art. She produces work for both domestic and commercial spaces.

Today she lives in her family home in Leicester with her husband, Eric and their wonderfully devoted dog Teddy.

http://jaliart.com/

INTRODUCTION

FOR NOREEN 1916 – 2010

Today the term dementia is in the news wherever we look. We are all expected to live longer than ever before, with better diets and improved living conditions – and with medical breakthroughs to sustain us, it is anticipated that memory impairment will have a greater and greater impact on our society as our population ages. We must develop new tactics to cope with this 21st century scourge.

This book offers tactics for dealing with the early stages of dementia, the time when both sufferer and carer are coming to terms with the fact that their lives will be different from now on. But the period following diagnosis is not all doom and gloom – only a period of adjustment, a new stage of life. It is a time to heighten the senses, and to use them to help clarify what is going on around us.

Our senses are great mechanisms that help us attune to our surroundings. They heighten our awareness and open the doorways for better communication.

Consider some of our sayings: "taking time to smell the roses"; "the light at the end of the tunnel"; "a touch of magic"; "the sound of silence"; "a taste of honey". We are always using words to communicate the importance of our five senses.

We should always open our minds to allow our senses to become as efficient as possible. They can be a tremendous help to us if memory impairment occurs.

Dementia is a snake – moving in a variety of directions, sometimes quickly and sometimes slowly and silently to make our lives difficult. But we can understand it; we can make sense of it.

I spent many years with my aunt, whose memory impairment began in her 70s – and with the help and support of my husband and family, we tried to 'make sense' of the dementia journey until she died at the great age of 94.

"The Plateau" is a simple allegorical illustration of the sensory journey we made together.

The Plateau

It was a beautiful spring day. Noreen decided that she would go for a walk to take in the new life that was bursting out all over the countryside.

Close to her home was a hill where she and her late husband Harry had taken many long, happy walks in days gone by.

She found it difficult these days to climb to the top and absorb the views, but about three quarters of the way up, the hill plateaued out before the final ascent to the summit.

It would be ideal, thought Noreen, to follow the plateau around the hill and reflect on past times.

The walk up to the plateau was relatively easy, though she did notice that she had become quite breathless and that certain things were just not as they used to be.

The first part of the walk was lovely. The birds wheeled their intricate patterns in the sky above her; a plane travelled across the blue arc leaving a sun dappled, silver-white vapour trail; people waved to her from the summit, some of whom she knew from the village, others whom she did not recognise – but she waved back happily.

What she did not notice was that the path around the plateau was, almost imperceptibly at first, leading downhill.

Suddenly she felt that the people on the summit were further away. The birds were less easy to see, the crystal clear quality of the light fading. The first stirrings of anxiety coursed through her body.

The path became stonier and more difficult to negotiate. By now the people on the summit were unrecognisable, undifferentiated specks on the landscape.

She reached the bottom; here the stream that flowed through the village had become a hissing, foaming snake as the water was forced through a narrow gap. The light faded more and Noreen stood there cold, confused and tired. She had no idea what to do.

She felt a familiar touch as a hand rested on her shoulder and a perfume filled the air, familiar and comforting. She turned around and saw a warm, welcoming smile. A soft voice in her ear said, "Come on Nor Nor – let's go home for tea."

The story illustrates the confusion that a person suffering from dementia may experience even though the surroundings may be very familiar. Confusion may take over very quickly but, with gentle reassurance from a loved one, during the early stages, it is possible to regain confidence and continue with a normal pattern of life.

Chapter 1
WHAT ARE THE BEST TACTICS FOR DEALING WITH DEMENTIA?

Going Up The Snakes And Down The Ladders

When we hear the word dementia, we tend to freeze and think about instant life-changing ways of "losing it", of "going gaga", but let's stop for a minute: the term is dementia, not *dim*entia. It means that the memory is starting to become a little impaired, not that our mind is instantly erased or we have become stupid, dim.

Life doesn't stop at diagnosis – but nevertheless we should begin putting certain strategies into place to help us along the next leg of our dementia journey.

So what should we do? Well, here's my philosophy: -

Life is like being an actor
In a play
First learn all of your lines
Really thoroughly
Then throw away the script
And
Ad lib all the way
Going up the snakes
And
Down the ladders

Why Down The Ladders And Up The Snakes?

Dementia has no set rules; the rules change like shifting sand, and so we must learn to compose new rules in order to make life as comfortable as possible.

Everyone is different, with differing needs and no two scenarios may be the same. We must change the rules to fit our own personal needs and wants to allow stability for both the sufferer and carer.

You must change the rules to suit you, yours and your lifestyle.

Have you ever read the Harry Potter books or seen the films? Who would have thought that the game of *quidditch*, that doesn't fit into any of our preconceived ideas of sport, would now have a strong following at Oxbridge with more and more teams taking part?

And would anyone living twenty years ago have believed that lying on a tin tray and skeltering around an ice track would be part of any Olympic games? Evolution. Everything changes, so all we can do is go with the flow.

So let's go up the snakes and down the ladders. Adapting and changing the rules is, in my view, the best tactic for living with the early stages of dementia.

Be Smart

If a sportsperson attempts to become the best at their given sport, they must adopt strategies in order to constantly improve and be at the top of their game.

A tried and tested method of charting performance, which you may have heard of, is the SMART principal – an acronym for the 5 steps of improving performance through *S*pecific/ *M*easurable/ *A*chievable/ *R*ecorded and *T*ime-phased goals.

The SMART principles may be applied to sport, business and in fact to any learning situation.

As a former P.E (Physical Education) teacher, I related many of the references below to sports performance but sport is analogous to dementia. In both we try to stay on top of our game, to go forward, stabilize and improve.

I give examples on how each aspect of the principal can be adapted to dementia. Remember however to adapt it your needs and circumstances. Make it work for you.

SPECIFIC--training in sport should be applicable to the sport. For example there is no need to run marathons if you are a snooker player however concentration exercises are a must. (Concentration exercises would they not be specific to those experiencing memory impairment?)

MEASURABLE--we must be able to track progress e.g. as an archer tracks the number of golds hit during each set of flights. With dementia it would be tracking memory lapses.

ACHIEVABLE-- One sport compliments the other. We can expect a fencer to achieve better reaction times if he/she plays other reaction sports as well, such as squash. In dementia we must try to keep the tracks of memory joined by initiating thought patterns to be channeled to help the sufferer be more coherent.

RECORDED/REALISTIC--we must set relevant tasks. A boxer, for example, trains in distance running and skipping and keeps a record of times and speeds as well as distances – a must for stamina and reaction. With dementia we look for relevant therapies to encourage lucidity and self-worth, such as art therapy.

TIME-PHASED--A sportsperson will have deadlines to reach certain goals e.g. reaching Olympic standard speed to be eligible for the 100m. sprint. With dementia we must pace what we do, keeping calm and adding lots of repetition.

So if we look at therapies for helping dementia sufferers we must answer these questions, as Kipling did:
Who--the sufferer or carer
What--do we want to accomplish--better memory links or relaxation or exercise + many more
Where--will these therapies take place--at home--with a group etc.
When--will we use these therapies--when appropriate/at specific times
Why--do we want to do this--to improve the quality of life

Chapter 2
DO YOU UNDERSTAND THE SUFFER'S PERSPECTIVE?

Have you ever seen a child who lacks spatial awareness try to play a team game on a court or a field? As a former P.E teacher, I have. They move around with no concept of no concept of the whereabouts of others participating in the game.

They become frustrated; eventually their teammates refuse to interact with them. The result is isolation and, at times, aggression, as they do not fit in; they are literally "out of step".

Put that same child behind a table tennis table and suddenly a game unfolds. Reason being --- the space is narrowed and the game takes place in a much more confined area eliminating the confusion of trying to operate with lots of other team members at the same time.

They may be not necessarily at championship standard. Yet the result: the child's self-esteem is raised, with he or she functioning within a sporting area and interacting with the person on the other side of the table.

They are no longer outcast but included and competent. Now that's what I call a good result.

Dementia is similar. It changes all our 'spatial awareness,' whether we suffer from it ourselves or are living with and/or caring for someone who suffers from it.

So again, we must learn to adapt, evolve and sometimes change the rules of the game by going 'up the snakes and down the ladders'.

It never hurts to change the rules if it makes the game flow better – in the case of dementia adapt your lifestyle to get the best out it, even if it seems a little non-conventional. If it works for you, go for it.

We are constantly changing, evolving. Our lives are a changing tapestry of events and memory. We store each moment in our memory, to recall at later dates - when we play them back almost like a DVD, to relive sensory experiences and clothe them in mental pictures. We all enjoy reliving our 'feel-good factor' moments.

We are all sensory animals, responding all the time to sensory data: that touch, taste, that smell, that sound, that certain smile.

The following is an example of how a seemingly straightforward task for one person can be an obstacle course for another. It illustrates how our coping mechanisms vary and how solutions may be found to overcome these stumbling blocks. It has has helped me over the years in caring for those suffering from dementia, for example my aunt Noreen, and now helps me with the local community group that I run for those affected with dementia. It has also helped me as a carer to get over my own stumbling blocks – to open the shutters and see things more clearly.

Riding Along In My Automobile

I am a geographical dyslexic; I always have been. I'm frightened to read a map. They make no sense to me, and my worst nightmare is being asked to give directions.

The fact that I am so inept heightens my embarrassment and I become agitated. I am much, much better at finding places when I am on foot, when I have time to notice familiar surrounding and to feel safe within recognisable territory. I enjoy meeting and talking to people as I walk.

In fact I am an extremely sociable animal – *but* put me behind the wheel of a car moving at *a greater speed than walking*, unable to sense familiar sights, sounds and smells, and I am lost. Strip me of some of my senses and you erase my comfort zone – a mist descends over me. I am no longer happy or considerate. I am frustrated, anxious and unable to function normally.

My family find this hard to understand. To them the simple task of driving from A to B is natural and simple. To me, it is a mammoth feat of mental dexterity, mental dexterity which eludes me when I am asked to go to a place where I haven't driven before. Invariably, then, I turn into an ogre – irritable, angry and unable to take in any directions given to me. My palms sweat, and all that I want to do is get out of the car and walk away.

It's like trying to find my way out of a maze in the dark and without a torch. Confusion, lack of control and a knotted stomach are not a good mix. Personality is stripped away and fear takes hold. It is, as I've often referred to it, my PDT – Pre Driving Tension. But it was not the physical act of driving that does this to me. I know I am a good driver. It is the journey itself – the venturing into the *unknown*.

To elaborate, let me tell you something that happened to me recently and is still very fresh in my memory.

Now my husband and I seldom argue – *except*... well, let me tell you the story.

It was a lovely summer's evening. I had to travel to a shopping centre on the outskirts of Leicester, one I know well. Now, I feel relatively comfortable starting any journey from the family home in Leicester, where I've lived since I was a youngster. But as I was about to leave, my wonderful husband announced that he would be coming with me.

"My secretary's left a present in the office," he said. "I've promised to take it over to her, and she lives close to the shops, so it makes sense to go with you."

Panic buttons sounded. My heart went *Boom-Bang-A-Bang*.

"Okay." I snapped back at him, "but only if you sit in the back and don't say a word!"

We set off and, to be fair, he didn't say a word – but as I was driving along my *'strange'* route (knowing that he would be wondering why I was not going there directly, as he would have done), I felt his eyes burning with disbelief into the back of my neck. My palms were sweating, but as promised he didn't say a word.

That was until we reached a major intersection. The main road out of Leicester to the M1 motorway is flanked by two service roads both of which lead to the shopping centre. The logical route to take was along the inner service road, but I felt more comfortable in the outer one as the thought of getting near the motorway terrified me.

I had crossed the main road to get to the service road when it happened.

"Where are you going, Jane?" he bellowed from the back. "You're going the wrong way!"

My panic became palpable. The rest of the journey was a nightmare.

Eventually I parked the car, got out and threw the keys at him. He drove home.

Four days later an official looking envelope dropped through our letterbox. It was from Leicestershire Constabulary. I had been filmed travelling at 42 mph in a 30 mph zone. A £60 fine and points on my licence!

When my loving husband arrived home, I showed it to him.

"This is all your fault," I snapped. "It was last Friday on the way to the shopping centre, if you hadn't been with me it wouldn't have happened."

"Don't be silly," he said. "If you had gone the right way it wouldn't have happened."

"Well, I'll take the points," I shouted, "but you can pay the fine. It's only fair."

And, bless him, he did.

That night I was reminded again what a trial it was, my having little or no sense of direction – for me, and for the people around me. I was comfortable doing it my way (well, almost) but knowing that my way appeared stupid to others made me miserable. But the most important thing was that I landed up in the right place not by going along the conventional route, but by going up the snakes and down the ladders.

It is so important for those whose mental ability is not as it once was to feel comfortable with the way that their lives are going – and as a carer, to have the insight into their confusion. Devise the best ways of dealing with it, which helps both of you to function comfortably.

Remaining calm and not conveying irritation to the sufferer is one of the best things that a carer can do. As a carer, it's important to allow the sufferer to ride his or her own road with confidence.

After years of behaving like this so uncharacteristically, a totally different person when travelling to a new destination, I discovered the satnav – or rather it found me, as my husband bought me a new car with an inbuilt system.

It was alien to me at first – a strange voice from the dashboard slowly, precisely and without a hint of irritation directing me to my destination. If I made a mistake, the voice calmly took me along a new route, with no annoyance at my ineptitude.

I started by putting in postcodes of places, short distances away and already familiar to me, just to make sure the voice knew what it was at. Slowly but surely I became more comfortable and confident travelling longer distances, and recently made a 50 mile round trip, for me it was mammoth.

I now personalise my satnav by calling her Vera – a nod to Vera Lynn, the Forces sweetheart, who made so many people feel safe and secure during wartime with her songs of hope.

Familiarisation works wonders for confidence, and for me the first journey with Vera was a triumph – "A small step for most but a giant leap for my kind". Now "I've been everywhere, man".

Vera is now my small voice of calm. She is my navigational carer. She doesn't get angry with me. She points me in the right direction calmly and logically and I am comfortable in her presence. I trust her.

How important is that to us all in our everyday life, particularly for those who have dementia – not to crush but to create stability?

Vera and I now co-habit very well in the car. I cannot function without her and she needs me in order to perform her 'job'. She is my carer in the car and she suffers my inadequacies with infinite patience – for which she has my undying gratitude and thanks. So akin is this to dealing with the early stages of dementia.

Chapter 3
CAN YOU MAKE 'SENSE' OF YOUR TIME TOGETHER?

Making Sense Of It

Dementia is an identity thief. It tries its hardest to steal our memories and debilitate our physical capacities. We have to put in place our own personal alarm systems to try to keep ourselves safe for as long as possible from that which tries to strip away our very essence.

During its early stages, as both carer and sufferer try to make sense of the rules by which the dementia game plays, it is important to stimulate the mental palaces that we have built in our lifetime. To recall happy family memories, times spent with loved ones; to slow down life's pace a little and take time to smell the roses.

Don't shut your self away. Confront the problem together; invent your own strategies to cope. Don't be afraid to ask for help. Others near you may well have gone up the snakes and down the ladders – so find them, talk to them. Engage.

We all at times experience mental blocks, but somehow manage to jump over them, often with the help of an outside support. Dementia requires its own particular springboard – not a 'one size fits all' device, but more of a bespoke design tailored to individual needs.

For a gymnast, pacing the right run-up and landing on the correct take-off point is to a great extent a matter of trial and error. We must practice, practice, and must approach the pathway with confidence. This is the way to approach the dementia game.

And to begin to make sense of this game, either as sufferer or carer, we must start with our senses.

Here are a few 'sensible' approaches that worked for me and my aunt Noreen.

Activities For Our Senses

Our five senses – sight, touch, taste, hearing and smell – are vital to us in our everyday life. We are all aware that if one (of more) of our senses is not functioning fully, the other senses rally around to compensate – for example, if a person loses their sight then hearing and awareness of smells may increase in sensitivity.

Our memory is our sixth sense and if that is impaired as it is in the case of dementia, then other 5 senses become more vital – helping us cope with everyday life and recall.

TASTE

Let's look first at our sense of taste. We are all urged to eat more fresh fruit and vegetables and to avoid unhealthy food but sometimes eating the naughty but nice options can release endorphins. Certain foods like ice cream and chocolate make us smile. They are widely believed to release endorphins that induce the "feel good factor" and can also trigger memories of happy events.

Use this to your advantage.

As an adult, have you ever tried eating a sherbet fountain through a liquorice straw, feeling the tingling in your nose as it hits your olfactory senses and giggling to yourself as you recall your childhood days? If not, try it, and see if it brings back happy childhood memories.

Sufferers and carers - enjoy meals together. Make them a relaxing and sociable time. No one needs to count the minutes, so avoid rushing, and make time for the digestive processes to do their work. Enjoy the experience. Make meals an everyday happy event. Make meals colourful and try to stick set times as routine is important for the dementia sufferer.

Enjoy the pleasure that these times in the day bring. It keeps the appetite healthy.

The colour of food can also brighten the plate and the mood. Presenting food is an art form, so whether serving a sandwich or a three course meal – knowthat we taste with our eyes before we eat.

And when mealtimes are done, work together to wash dishes or stack a dishwasher. These jobs need to be done, and at the same time allows to sufferer to stay involved. It continues their feeling of self worth and being useful.

SMELL

Second, let's consider our sense of smell.

Weather permitting, try to go for a walk each day. It doesn't matter if you follow the same route each time – in fact, this may be better, as familiarity and routine reinforces security for those with dementia.

The walk is the time to look for things that we may have missed when we hurry. Notice the little corners where flowers may be blooming. Talk, relax and perhaps sometimes notice together the "the little petunia in an onion patch".

Beauty is all around, so look for it. Heighten your senses by noticing the smells that accompany the seasons – light and fragrant spring, heady and pungent summer, woody and smoky autumn, crisp and clean winter.

Here's an example of how our senses cleverly work together to evoke memory.

Have you ever, while walking on a November evening, inhaled the wonderfully smoky smell of bonfire, which have triggered memories of Bonfire Nights of yesteryears – when fireworks were an amazing array of light, colour and sound?

I remember once walking with Noreen on such an evening. We reminisced, through that smoky scent, the types of fireworks that she would buy for me when I was young– the traffic lights, volcanoes, sparklers, rockets and jumping jacks. Then recalled their familiar sounds - 'crackles,' 'whizzes,' 'bangs' and 'pops.'

We both opened our 'bonfire' memory room to relive past times, and so were using mental pictures, sounds and smells to bring the past to the fore. In fact, Noreen requested jacket potatoes and sausages for supper that night – as we always ate these on Bonfire Night.

All these type of activities to do with our senses help us to relive the sensations that link to our memory, so keeping it unlocked, wide open and accessible for as long possible.

HEARING

Third, use your sense of hearing to its best advantage. Again allow your senses the time to listen out for the sounds of your surroundings. Keep things real – the singing of the birds, the laughter of children playing, "the sound of silence" in the company of those you are with.

We all listen out for triggers to spark off conversation in the company of family, friends and new acquaintances, making for an easy conversational flow. The same principle applies when in the dementia zone.

Our memory strands are like train tracks, sometimes, as with normal track lines they can crack and disjoin, causing disruption to journeys. Our mental faculties are very similar. Dementia causes the train lines of our thoughts to pull apart, and we must devise tactics to pull them together, to ease confusion.

Listen out for things that can help to "pull the train tracks" of memory together.

So some of things that you can do are ask questions such as, "Do you remember that concert we went to together where...?" Use certain lines in favourite films which may be relevant to both of you like "Play it again, Sam" from the film Casablanca (*did you know it was never actually said*).

When I was a child, family Christmases together were special times – times of laughter, song and reminiscence. Every member of the family had a song that they would sing on Christmas Eve.

My father's was "The Little Boy That Santa Claus Forgot", my mother's was "Alice Blue Gown", mine was "The Little Drummer Boy" and my aunt's for some reason was "This Little Duck That Waddled Upstairs". Noreen and I would often recall these times, with great clarity.

So remember your special times-- replay the scenes and sounds, and if you can, sing. The words of songs stay with us throughout most our lifetime, and when recalled evokes happy memories.

TOUCH

Touch is an extremely powerful sense. We all thrive on contact to make us feel part of any society, big or small.

Our sense of touch relates to our sense of belonging. Holding hands with or a touch on the face from someone we know, someone who cares, can mean the difference between isolation and inclusion. We all need to feel that we belong.

There are times when I was caring for my aunt that I knew that she felt confused and could not piece everything together. At times I would sit and hold her hands, and we would do nothing more than sit quietly in each other's company.

The warmth and comfort of a loving touch fulfills a basic human need. We feel close and "special"—loved and needed, like we belong.

Noreen and I used hand massage – with lavender cream, not oils, which we found too messy. Not only would I massage my aunt's hands (followed by nail filing and polishing), but she would massage *my* hands too – showing that she cared for me, and so that she was needed *by* me. And she was.

Massaging the hands stimulates the blood flow as well as giving comfort. And, of course, our hands are always on show – so the "feel-good" factor is doubly enhanced, as looking good helps us to feel good about ourselves.

As part of our touch therapy, I developed my artwork, using crystals and craft products to produce tactile art. My aunt was able to use her sense of touch to feel the work. The mental imagery evoked by this touch gave her added confidence to her conversation with me about my art.

Another fun touch exercise we used was pastry and biscuit making – kneading pastry people, sugar filled "mice" and fruit shaped biscuits, which we would then cover in coloured icing. Again we worked together, often laughing over the "disasters " but also doing something useful, as my grandchildren loved to eat them. Try it, it's good fun.

SIGHT

Look at things with a sense of wonder. Enjoy all the colour and shade that the world has to offer us. Surround yourself with colour. Colour can stimulate emotion. Fill your surroundings, to improve your wellbeing.

Look into Feng Shui and choose artwork and decorations that will make your home feel happy and secure. Use colour to enhance mood. We used my artwork, alive with colour and crystals, to enhance our walls and so induce the "feel-good" factor, to make our home seem "right". My aunt chose the colours that pleased her and we surrounded ourselves with images of glittering butterflies, owls, horses, peacocks and gardens. She loved these, as she said they "filled her with joy".

Choosing the right coloured clothes to wear was also important to my aunt's sense of wellbeing. To improve her mood, we chose bright colours – greens, lavenders, oranges – and she really enjoyed the feeling that she was always "presentable. She would often check her appearance in the mirror, a good sign as it proved that she was taking an interest. It was good to see how it improved her mood.

We also enjoyed, and I still do, keeping lots of colourful fruit and flowers around the house. These are always a spirit lifter and make the home environment feel welcoming to others. I believe that the scent, sounds and sights of a home are important, as these are the elements that make it welcoming.

Chapter 4
WHAT ABOUT YOU?

How I Overcame My Frustration As A Carer

"The Treasured Crystal"

I remember a day when I, as carer, became quite irritated with my aunt's behaviour – and then something happened which helped me understand what was happening to my aunt. It helped me see through the dementia and into the person that I had loved. So gave me more patience when she was needy.

Here's the story.

Several years ago my husband bought me a beautiful crystal, oval in shape and itself covered with alum crystallite, except for one flat shaved area from which the inner, complex crystal could be viewed.

I kept this treasured object on a wooden shelf in my bedroom, so that I could see it each time I entered the room – although if I'm honest, more of the alum than the crystal was on display.

One day while cleaning the shelf, I accidently knocked my beloved crystal onto the floor, where it smashed and broke into six irregular pieces. I was distraught.

I carefully picked up the pieces, worried all the while that the jagged edges might cut my hands, and replaced them on the shelf.

For a little while I just stared at them, not sure if I should discard them, as I knew that I could never put them back together again. My crystal could never again be perfect. The object that I had treasured so much in the past was no longer complete.

And that was my initial thought – that a small corner of my world was gone forever.

I stood there feeling angry with myself for allowing this to have happened. I should have been more careful, I told myself. I could have prevented it. I felt guilty.

But as I stood there lamenting what had happened, a shaft of light poured through the window onto the fractured pieces, making each piece glisten independently. At that moment I realised the beauty lay not just in the whole crystal, but within each individual facet, too.

As I looked deeper, I saw that every piece was a beautiful object in its own right. Each had its own merits. The pieces were no longer regular and their surfaces were certainly rougher than before – but they were still exquisite. Still well worth cherishing.
It dawned on me that this was a metaphor for my aunt at the moment. Her personality not as it was, changing, yet fragments of her old self still remained, which comforted me. It helped me to cope.

So remember: although dementia may sometimes appear to fragment our personality, the person we love is still there.

But what can we do to try to control this apparent memory fragmentation?

Here are a few ideas.

Keeping Track

I need my diary; it is my survival tool, lest I forget.

I found when caring for my aunt that our own week-at-a-glance diaries were invaluable.

Planning our diaries was a pleasant activity on a Sunday afternoon, and it helped us to see what each of us was up to. Because I love colour, I found it useful to put my movements in green (my favourite colour) and hers in red (her favourite colour). Each was then easily comprehensible 'at a glance'.

(Diary-keeping was also a good and practical way for my aunt to continue to use her handwriting skills).

Each day my aunt could know 'at a glance' where I was and what I was doing – she just had to look for the green words. This helped her, whenever she started to feel panicked about my whereabouts. It was her security blanket. Similarly, it helped me to know where she should be and who she should be with, whenever I needed to contact her quickly.

This diary setting may well work for you. It's not unlike the school timetable or the family planner. If more than one of the family is going to help in the caring role, each can use a specific colour – but keep the colour constant and choose wisely. By this I mean: make sure that each colour chosen stands out from the others. Do not use similar colours, like purple and lavender. Keep things as clear as possible, visually.

And very importantly: remember to all give yourself enough time to work, rest and play.

Variety Is The Spice Of Life

We all need some structured repetition in our lives – again, it is familiarity, which produces confidence.

If we look at the structure of a school timetable, we can see that consistency is needed for both pupil and teacher. Neither cope too well if the rhythm of the school day is altered without notice. Both feel disturbed and unprepared, as their mind-set has, unexpectedly, to readjust.

Yet to fill our days, we need not only repetition but variety – the former to give a sense of familiarity, the latter to alleviate boredom.

We had routine – like set meal times etc. And to add variety to our days Noreen and I visited local farm parks. We had tea parties. We joined local social clubs, many of them inexpensive and enjoyable. The members of my support group also really enjoy meeting the new people who come in to entertain us each month – some of our members are now learning to play the ukulele since a musical group played for us – something that we would not have thought of before.

Simple things, for a change, can be a great pick-me-up: a train journey through the countryside to a different town, a day trip out on a bus, going out into the local community to support amateur dramatic groups. Use what works for you.

The Importance Of A Comfortable Home Environment

My aunt lived in our family home with us – a colourfully mismatched home. Antiques sit comfortably next to bric-a-brac; fresh flowers scent the rooms. Cushions are everywhere. Reed diffusers spill out favourite aromas.

My advice here is to create a setting in which you and yours feel comfortable and calm, as we spend a great deal of time in our homes. Try also to keep things constant. Do not keep changing furniture around. Keep settings familiar. Remember that consistency is key to keeping those with dementia calm – there's no need to add to their confusion.

You as carer also need your own private space. We found it vital to create our own zones for 'me time'; spaces to read, listen to music or just relax. Take time to organise your home so that this essential breathing space is accommodated.

Chapter 5
I'VE NOT LOST MY MIND, IT'S BACKED UP ON DISK SOMEWHERE

We live in a computer-generated age, an age of instant answers. But as people we are not instant; we need time to process, to work through questions to reach a goal.

We shouldn't become automatons. We are all unique, so let's allow our individualism to shine through; we don't have to be perfect, or even to strive for perfection. Sometimes it is all right to play all the right notes in the 'wrong' order. Didn't we all love Morecombe and Wise for that?

Remember that at school, it took many months and many mistakes to learn our times table. As a former teacher, I am all too aware that learning and recall processes are different for all of us. Some require visual learning aids, for others colour is a key factor; some like to acquire knowledge by rote while others need several routes to follow. All our minds have their own intrinsic maps to learning, whether our minds are functioning normally or beginning to fragment.

These are light bulb moments, the triggers to releasing memory.

The old adage that Rome was not built in a day certainly rings true. Search for your own triggers to help you through your days. Finding them may be a matter of trial and error – but are well worth searching for.

How Triggers For them, Can Help You

A dementia sufferer can quickly become confused and anxious when an unexpected event occurs. But let's not forget that all of us, in stressful situations, may close down the shutters, put out the lights and refuse to absorb sad or hurtful information. Our brains have inbuilt defence mechanisms to protect us from stress and harm.

Dementia sufferers need to find a point of focus, a gentle voice to calm confusion and fear.

I should give here a brief potted history of my aunt Noreen to show how a trigger helped us in a very difficult situation.

My aunt was widowed during World War II. She and her husband Harry were married in 1942 and he was lost in active service in the jungles of Burma in 1943. Her sister Nellie had suffered similarly. Nellie's husband George was in the Navy and was lost when his ship, the HMS Prince of Wales, was sunk.

Nellie and George had a son, my cousin David, born in 1941. David never met his father. So Nellie and our large family, especially Noreen, brought up David and she viewed him as a son.

David did extremely well academically, studying at Cambridge University and subsequently working as a professor of archaeology at Manchester University, where he was instrumental in the excavation of a Bronze Age archaeological site, Flag Fen in Peterborough. Noreen was immensely proud of his achievements, particularly Flag Fen.

One Spring I had to be away for the weekend. I was reluctant to go but my husband insisted that it would be a good break for me and that he was happy to care for Noreen during that time.

But none of us anticipated how the weekend would develop.

Sadly David had contracted stomach cancer, and while we were all aware of the severity of his situation, none of us envisaged that the call would come that weekend to say he had died.

Eric, my husband, telephoned me to let me know, and we agonised for a while about whether he should tell Noreen then, or wait until I arrived home. We decided that she should know immediately, and with some trepidation he went to her and delivered the news.

He described to me how her face had become expressionless and her eyes 'glazed over'. For two hours she paced about the house, stopping on many occasions to ask, "Eric, who is it that has died?" "David," he would reply. "Your nephew David. George and Nellie's son." But nothing seemed to penetrate her veil of confusion. Then after much repetition of the question and answer routine, Eric gave a slightly different answer. "Your nephew David, Aunt Nor, who excavated Flag Fen."

The veil lifted. "Oh, not David!" She cried. Calmness was restored. A natural grief surfaced; she sat down in her chair, drank sweet tea, and with sparkling eyes started to speak affectionately of David.

Strange as it may seem the words Flag Fen were the keys to unlock the memory, causing the agitation to subside and a more natural sadness to arise. The memory required a trigger.

When I returned home the next day, Eric told me what had happened. I found my aunt calm, philosophical and loving.

The lessons that Eric and I had learnt together during her illness had stood him in good stead in dealing with that unexpected and difficult evening.

He realised that, above all, he needed to stay calm, patient and relaxed in a situation where it would have been easy to become irritated. Any irritation on his part would only have exacerbated the situation for both of them, increasing her fear and bewilderment.

The His use of the words Flag Fen was in a sense a lucky break, but taught us both that in similar situations a trigger, a link, is needed to join together the chain of memory, and is of paramount importance.

Life Is Rich, Enjoy It

During the early stages of dementia, it is important to keep things in perspective. The sufferer will at times experience lapses of memory, and then feels upset and frustrated that this has happened.

The carer will naturally feel apprehension and wonder if they are up to the job. Both have an important role to play in "the game". Remember wherever possible to be positive – both of you.

This isn't always easy, I know – but it's essential to continue life as 'normally' as possible. It is also essential for both sufferer and carer to maintain the feeling of self worth, to feel secure and not believe that life stops here; it doesn't. It's just a new and different phase. Finding triggers that help is very important now to keep memory tracks joined for as long as possible.

Chapter 6
IS THEIR ANY SCIENCE TO THESE ACTIVITIES?

Endorphins Rule

Endorphins are produced in the pituitary gland, brain and nervous system. They are what give us a buzz after exercising. They are mathematical do-gooders and they love to multiply. The better we are feeling about ourselves, the more they multiply. So bring them on. The more the merrier.

Endorphins produce the feel good sensations that we all experience from time to time. They boost our self-esteem. They reduce stress. They make us walk tall. They are excellent allies to have on our side. So what can we do to keep a rich supply of these little helpers? Well, we can do plenty. And we tried many therapeutic therapies and came up with our own game-plan.

1. Laughter Therapy

"Laughter is the best medicine," as is often quoted. Today laughter therapy has been introduced to help treat certain medical conditions[1]. Laughter is also a deflective. It helps us forget the stresses of the day for a while. The more we laugh, the better our perspective on life and the better our sense of wellbeing.

Noreen and I would laugh regularly at some of the silly things we would do during the day.

There is a scene in the movie "The Sound of Music" where Maria is teaching the Von Trapp children to sing. While in the marketplace, the youngest child tries to juggle with two tomatoes, one of which falls on the floor and squashes. The little girl begins to cry, but Maria shakes a finger at her and smiles. Immediately the girl responds with a laugh – one small act of kindness changing a negative to a positive in moments.

Minor tragedies like the squashed tomato occur all of the time. Think, 'so what?' Laugh and the world will laugh with you. Laughter therapy is good for all of us.

The brain regulates laughter. When we laugh, we exercise the diaphragm that is positive exercise. When we giggle together, we can feel part of a group. Laughter turns isolation into inclusion. Medical research acknowledges the power of laughter in improving life of patients with chronic illnesses.[2]

Other studies suggest that laughter helps improve memory, well-being and alertness. Perhaps instead of "an apple day keeps the doctor away", we should say that "laughter a day keeps the doctor away."[3]

So spread the love.

2. Physical Exercise

---

[1] Studying the biology of hope: An interview with Lee S. Berk, DrPH, MPH. Interview by Sheldon Lewis. *Adv Mind Body. 2007 Summer;22(2):28-31*

"When we laugh endorphins are released from your brain cells. This makes you feel good and cheerful. Stress is reduced and your immune system boosted."
Laughter Aspirations 2011
http://www.laughteraspirations.co.uk/

[2] Academics from Oxford University published research demonstrating that continuous laughter significantly increases people's pain threshold by as much as 10%. *Oxford University Press/ Royal Society. September 2011*

[3] Alternative Therapies in Health & Medicine . Nov/Dec 2010, Vol. 16 Issue 6, p56-64. 9p. Mora-Ripoll, Ramon

Exercise is a great endorphin releaser. My aunt, in her younger days, was a prolific walker, at least eight miles a day – and for us, taking long walks together always made our moods lighter.

The hot cup of tea when we got back would taste even better after a walk – and so would the cold gin and tonic.

Of course it doesn't have to be walking, any exercise will do (we also had a skipping rope each). A favourite sport, housework and gardening are all good too.

For a while I did Tai Chi, which I practiced at home. My aunt would try to copy me with mostly hilarious consequences, and a fit of the giggles would invariably follow. The laughs we shared were good, honest and endorphin-rich.

Because of Tai Chi, I would also practice gentle meditation and breathing exercises – a great way to de-stress, and for my aunt a new form of exercise to learn.

3. Music

And while we're talking about exercise, let's not forget music therapy. Music also triggers joy and releases those feel-good chemicals: listening, playing and of course singing.

Music is extremely therapeutic; it can stimulate, calm and stir memory. It has power – it can make us want to dance, reflect, sing, tap our feet.

Do you recall the scene in the film "love actually" when Hugh Grant as the Prime Minister danced across the landing of number 10 when he heard "Jump" by Girls Allowed on the radio. It changed his state of mind from stress into a more relaxed happy mode. Music can do the same for most of us.

Listen to some music and dance around the house. Exercise DVDs encourage us to keep moving – sometimes my aunt and myself could be seen dancing the Gay Gordons in the garden. Or mix within social groups in your own community, such as local walking clubs, choirs or afternoon tea dances.

Singing also releases those wonderful endorphins. It helps with confidence and the words of songs stay locked in our memory for a tremendously long time

And, at times, we all need to rest, to recover our energy and our thoughts. Both of you, remember: take some "time out" when you need it.

Pet Therapy

Let's also not forget the value of pet therapy for all. Pets can lift spirits, reduce loneliness, provide comfort, lower anxiety and can also improve social, emotional and cognitive function[4].

Peter Pop

For my aunt, Peter Pop was pet therapy. Peter was a goldfish. He had been won at the fair by one of my nephews, Tom, who really didn't want him. Peter was not expected to live: Tom had brought him round in a soggy plastic bag, tied at the top and he – the goldfish that is – looked like he wasn't long for this world.

My aunt, however, had other ideas "He's a survivor," she announced as she filled up a washing up bowl with tepid water and placed him in it." I'll call him Peter Pop." We were all astonished at her interest in him.

"Why that name, Nor Nor?" I asked her.

"Well, I like the name Peter – and the bubbles he blows go pop at the top of the water."

I couldn't argue with that logic.

Peter survived the night and the next day in the washing up bowl, and my aunt fed him little pieces of dried bread – he truly was a survivor. We had to find a more permanent and more suitable home for him, and so I duly brought home an old bell-jar (and some fish food from the shops). Noreen carefully washed the jar, filled it with water and put it on the sideboard, Peter's new home. She loved him, buying him water plants and "toys," and it proved very relaxing for her to watch him swim. To this day Peter Pop has a special place in the hearts of the family.

A Stroke Of Luck

The power of the pet is immense. So important is it now deemed to have comforting contact with animals that 'cat cafes' have opened up all over the world, providing people with feline companionship while they have a cup of coffee. The cafes originated in Japan and are filled with a variety of cats for customers to stroke while they are there.

The American Veterinary Medical Association suggested in 2013 that pet therapy can aid progress towards goals in human physical, social, emotional and cognitive functions. It was certainly true for Noreen, who grew to love a scruffy little dog, as this story demonstrates.

I have always loved animals, my aunt not so much until Peter Pop – but she came, by accident, to develop a deep bond with a puppy, now a mature dog, our much-loved Teddy Tuppence.

---

[4] Margo A. Halm, *The Healing Power of the Human-Animal Connection*, American Journal of Critical Care July 2008 vol. 17 no. 4 373-376

As a family we decided (rather strongly influenced by me) that having a dog about the house would be a good idea, and so we went in search of our chosen Lassie. However, by a twist of fate, a scruffy little puppy found us.

We visited a farm where puppies of Westie origin were supposed to be for sale but when we got there all of the advertised puppies had been sold-"All I have left is this one," we were told by a rather unsavory owner and with that he took us to a shed, a very dirty shed, with only torn up newspaper on the floor and he brought out a forlorn looking white and apricot puppy of very mixed breed.

He put the puppy on the floor--it did not move--we clapped our hands--it did not move. We thought that this scruffy little flea infested (obvious) animal was both blind and deaf and on the brink of death. Surely we should have nothing to do with it.

Then it happened--Noreen decided that he should be picked up (he obviously had had very little human contact in his short life)--Well she held him and he put his head on her shoulder--that was that. Said scruffy one came home with us and became our beloved Teddy.

The comfort that he gave to Noreen was immense, and the care that she showed to him was heartwarming. Today he's definitely "our boy" – also known as Doctor Dog.

Chapter 7
WHAT OTHER FUN ACTIVITIES ARE THERE TO DO IN THE EARLY STAGES OF DEMENTIA?

Exercise That Mind

We can all find physical exercises that work for us, but let's not forget about exercising the mind. In the early stages of dementia, encourage sufferers to keep abreast of the news. Read the papers, read books, perhaps try word searches or keeping a personal record diary.

And play games – card games, board games, made-up games – anything that you enjoy and that is mentally stimulating. We used to (and still do) play a lot of games with my grandchildren, who are 6 and 10.

This one is called Boy/Girl. A game we play at my community group with much hilarity and a considerable amount of cheating.

Take 10 categories and different letters like so;

CATEGORY	LETTER B
Boy	Brian
Girl	Bharti
Flower	Bluebell

Fruit	Blackberry
Tree	Birch
Country	Belgium
Animal	Bear
Bird	Blackbird
Colour	Blue
Song Title	Bye Bye Blues

Play in teams of two (two heads are better than one and both can jog each others memory).

If any team have put used the same word then only one point is scored, if none is duplicated then two points are scored (remember the maximum score is twenty points (my grandchildren are "very good" at getting twenty two points).

It's actually very good fun – it's inclusive, it causes a lot of laughter, it gets the "little grey cells" moving and it's easy to set up. All you need are pens and paper.

My aunt used to be a book-keeper and had a great grasp of mathematical principles, particularly times-tables. In fact, she was excellent at mental arithmetic. We would play times-table games with my grandchildren – a good learning experience for them and great for my aunt's self-esteem.

Of course any game may be adapted to suit the players. Change the rules to suit the level. Increase or decrease complexity. Adapt, change - up the snakes and down the ladders.

Happy House Of Colour

I am a great believer in the power of colour. As an artist, I feel that we should have in our homes pictures that please us and create a positive ambience. Remember that beauty is whatever you perceive it to be – not what other people imagine it to be.

I draw and paint what pleases me. I incorporate colours and crystals to lift spirits, to relax, to please. After all, don't we plant our gardens for the same reason, for colour, for appearance and for relaxation? Everything around us is an art form and appeals to our senses. The colours we chose to dress in, the wallpaper on our walls, the carpets on the floor, the curtains at the windows.

Colour therapy worked really well for Noreen and me. She, bless her, was "not an artist" (as she put it) and so I would draw for her. We made colouring books of birds, animals and gardens and together we would enjoy the relaxation that the colouring-in process lent us – me with my paints and Noreen with her felt-tips. I had done this sort of thing before with my mother when she was hit with depression, with positive outcomes.

Colour therapy is absorbing productive – and telling. My aunt, for example, had always loved the colour and aroma of lavender, but I also found, as her illness progressed, that she was using more blue, red and yellow. She found these colours comforting.

It is well known among colour therapists that the colour blue relates to the throat. It relates to self-expression the ability to communicate to our needs and requirements.

So with her use of the colour blue, I realized that Noreen was expressing that she wanted to be heard clearly. She was telling her story to me through colour.

Socialize

Now don't feel guilty, if you are caring for someone, about having some social life of your own – some "me time" is allowed. It's healthy for both of you. It alleviates any resentment that may build up. Remember, the sufferer will also feel guilty during this early stage if they think that they are holding you back.

Both carer and sufferer should be free to go out separately, and to use this time apart as breathing space. It will make the time spent together better as it will diminish stress. Both of you need to maintain ties with your friends. Remember that they understand you. They have known you for a long time. You are their "treasured crystal" – and they are yours.

Pursue activities you both enjoy, not necessarily together. It gives you something to talk about when you get home. Stay independent, both of you; don't crowd one another too much during the early stages.

Maintain your friendships as these will help both of you and them to cope better when times get hard.

The Power Of Friends

I have lots of friends, all totally different and all wonderful and considerate. With good friends, it's not always necessary to talk. Sometimes "the sound of silence" is, in itself, of immense comfort. Their presence is like a loving cuddle, reassuring and warming – like eating hot chips out of a paper bag on a winter's walk.

One of my sets of friends I have known for over forty years. We met while at college together, young, giggly and full of joie de vie. We now meet as a group only once a year as we are scattered around the country, but heart-ties remain strong.

I know that when we meet, for the first five or ten minutes, we look at each other and see the evidence of the years – but, after that, we once again are 21.

We laugh. We sometimes shed a tear for those we have lost, and then share a giggle. Eat chocolate (good for you, as it releases endorphins) and watch silly DVD's.

Being comfortable in each other's company eliminates stress, is relaxing and warming, essential for all of our well-being and particularly important for those dealing with dementia, to help maintain equilibrium.

FINAL REFLECTIONS

It is an intrinsic human need to feel that we belong. We're all a useful link in our society. Everyone has a gift that is special – so share yours with friends and family. Don't stand alone. Let dementia unite, not divide you.

Use every sense that you may have to enjoy life – stay close to those you care for, and be there for each other.

We all need "somebody to lean on". Keep the heart-ties strong.
At times reflect together.
At times sing together.
But, above all, laugh together.

And remember: it's never too late to make new friends. We are all part of a society, whether a large or small one; take each others' hands and go "UP THE SNAKES AND DOWN THE LADDERS".

Printed in Poland
by Amazon Fulfillment
Poland Sp. z o.o., Wrocław